Want to Know Your Idol?

Justin Bieber

 BY PAUL

WAYLAND

First published in 2013 by Wayland
Copyright © Wayland 2013

Wayland
338 Euston Road
London NW1 3BH

Wayland Australia
Level 17/207 Kent Street
Sydney, NSW 2000

Commissioning editor: Debbie Foy
Designer: Ray Bryant
Series editor: Camilla Lloyd

Dewey ref: 782.4'2164'092-dc23
ISBN: 978 0 7502 7930 7
10 9 8 7 6 5 4 3 2 1

Printed in UK
Wayland is a division of Hachette Children's Books,
an Hachette UK company

www.hachette.co.uk

The author and publisher would like to thank the following for allowing their
pictures to be reproduced in this publication: Cover and 63 © Ouzouonova/
Splash News/Corbis; 4 © BRENDAN MCDERMID/Reuters/Corbis; 6 © Gary
Stafford/Corbis; 13 © Fairchild Photo Service/Condé Nast/Corbis; 27 © Frank
Trapper/Corbis; 29 © Pete's Photo of Stratford/Splash/Splash News/Corbis;
44 © Rainer Jensen/dpa/Corbis; 51 © Joe Stevens./Retna Ltd./Corbis; 58 © Jason
Webber/Splash News/Corbis; 72 © Splash News/Corbis.

Want to know EVERYTHING there is to know about

JUSTIN BIEBER?

Then head this way to become a true Belieber...

He's risen from internet sensation to recording star – and all in the space of a few years. He's the boy from the 'burbs that rubs shoulders with the rich and famous. From second place in a local talent contest to singing for the President. Who is it?

It's the ...

AWARD-WINNING, TEEN SENSATION

Justin Bieber!

Justin's army of fans are called **Beliebers** and if you're reading this book you're either a confirmed Belieber already or you'd like to be one!

Discover loads of facts and trivia about Justin, who is rumoured to be singing with him in the future and what records he has broken. Find out which sports Justin likes to play, what makes him tick – and read about his amazing rags-to-riches life story!

On top of all that there are fiendish quizzes to test your Bieber knowledge, and loads of information on all of Justin's albums.

WANT TO KNOW
YOUR IDOL?

Well, turn the page Belieber and immerse yourself in all things Justin...

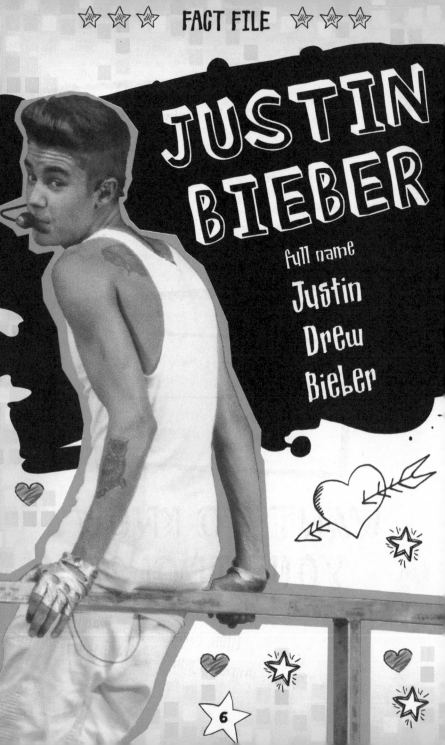

JUSTIN BIEBER

full name

Justin Drew Bieber

Date of birth: 1 March 1994

Place of birth: London, Ontario, Canada

Place he grew up: Stratford, Ontario

Where he lives now: Calabasas, California

Height: 170 cm (5 feet 6 inches)

Eye colour: Brown

Hair colour: Brown

Family

Father: Jeremy Jack Bieber

Mother: Patricia Mallette

Sister: Jazmyn Bieber

Brother: Jaxon Bieber

Languages spoken: English, French

Twitter name: @justinbieber

Fan clubs: http://bieberfever.com/

http://www.justinbiebermusic.com/

Top talents: Singing and dancing (obviously!)

Worst trait: Easily distracted and

gets bored quickly

☆ ☆ ☆ BIEBER BIO – BEFORE FAME! ☆ ☆ ☆

JUSTIN WAS BORN IN LONDON, ONTARIO ON 1 MARCH 1994. HIS MUM AND DAD WERE BOTH VERY YOUNG – HIS MUM, PATTIE, WAS ONLY EIGHTEEN WHEN SHE HAD HIM. UNFORTUNATELY HIS PARENTS DIDN'T STAY TOGETHER AND HIS DAD, JEREMY, LEFT WHEN JUSTIN WAS SMALL. THE GOOD NEWS WAS THAT THE FAMILY STAYED CLOSE; JUSTIN'S GRANDPARENTS HELPED RAISE HIM AND HIS DAD KEPT IN CONTACT.

Justin was pretty much like any other kid on the block. He **skateboarded** with his friends, enjoyed playing **football** and liked a game of chess. But what he kept hidden was his musical talent. He taught himself to play a few musical instruments and worked on some **dance moves**. He kept this quiet though so no one had any idea about what he could really do.

8

Justin's story proves that winning isn't everything. How come? Well his **YouTube** career started after coming second in a talent show back home in Stratford, Ontario. His mum put the video of the performance on YouTube and it started getting a lot of views; so Pattie put up more videos of Justin singing cover versions of acts such as Ne-Yo and Stevie Wonder. Soon they were attracting serious interest...

JUSTIN HAS 8 CARS SO IF YOU NEED WHEELS TO GET AROUND HE'S YOUR GO-TO GUY FOR COOL CARS! HERE ARE THE HIGHLIGHTS OF HIS SUPER-COOL COLLECTION:

CADILLAC CTS-V

NORMALLY THIS CADDY IS A BIG (IF A BIT BORING) CAR. JUSTIN HAS PIMPED HIS RIDE THOUGH SO IT LOOKS LIKE THE BATMOBILE!

Holy custom job, Beebman!

FISKER KARMA

THE SPORTS CAR FOR THE ECO-CONSCIOUS. JB GAVE IT HIS OWN STYLE WITH ANOTHER CUSTOM PAINT JOB. NOT BLACK THIS TIME – THE FISKER GOT A SUPER-SHINY CHROME LOOK!

SMART CAR

THIS TINY CAR IS IDEAL FOR CITY DRIVING AND JUSTIN'S MATT BLACK CUSTOM PAINT JOB GIVES HIS EXTRA SWAG ON THE STREET!

RANGE ROVER

IF THE SMART CAR IS FEELING A BIT POKEY, JUSTIN GIVES HIMSELF A BIT OF ROOM IN THIS POSH 4x4. THIS ONE HAS THE SAME PAINT JOB AS THE SMART CAR, BUT YOU'RE UNLIKELY TO GET THEM MIXED UP.

Justin has also been spotted driving matt black Ferraris and Porsches. He's also given a Segway a try, but we doubt they're as fast as those sports cars!

of course there's one set of wheels he's been riding for years

his skateboard!

11

A RECORD COMPANY MANAGER CALLED **SCOOTER BRAUN** WAS TRAWLING THE INTERNET LOOKING FOR NEW POP ACTS WHEN JUSTIN CAUGHT HIS ATTENTION. HIS TALENT WAS CLEAR TO SEE AND SCOOTER WAS IMPRESSED THAT JUSTIN WAS ALSO A SELF-TAUGHT MUSICIAN. SO SCOOTER GOT IN TOUCH WITH PATTIE, JUSTIN'S MOTHER...

Pattie was worried about exposing Justin to the pressure of the music business, but Scooter convinced her that he would take proper care of her son. Scooter flew Justin and Pattie to Atlanta to discuss things further.

When Justin arrived at Scooter's office who should be there in the car park?

USHER!

Better still, the R&B star was there to meet Justin! Usher was Scooter's business partner at the record label and hoped to convince Justin to sign. With one of his heroes on board it was a match made in heaven.

Once Justin was signed things started moving fast. In 2009 his first single was released. **One Time** did well and charted in over 30 countries. The first **My World** album followed and Justin became the first artist to have **seven singles** from a debut album reach the singles chart. Justin had arrived in style! The hits kept on coming and by the time **My Worlds 2.0** was released Justin was a major star. The album hit the number 1 spot in the US charts.

JUSTIN WAS NOW AN UNSTOPPABLE MUSIC MACHINE, SELLING OUT STADIUMS ACROSS THE GLOBE WHENEVER HE TOURED.

Justin and Usher

PATTIE MALLETTE

THE BIGGEST INFLUENCE IN JUSTIN'S LIFE HAS BEEN HIS MOTHER, PATTIE. WHEN SHE WAS YOUNGER PATTIE WAS A BIT OF A TEARAWAY AND BY THE AGE OF 18 SHE HAD A YOUNG SON, JUSTIN. SHE TOOK GOOD CARE OF HER BABY, WORKING HARD TO SUPPORT HIM AND HAS ALWAYS STOOD BY HIM. JUSTIN OFTEN TAKES HIS MUM TO AWARDS CEREMONIES AND SHE'S ALWAYS ON TOUR WITH HIM.

JAZMYN AND JAXON BIEBER

JAZMYN AND JAXON ARE JUSTIN'S HALF-SISTER AND HALF-BROTHER (ON HIS DAD'S SIDE). THEY ARE MUCH YOUNGER THAN HE IS, BUT JUSTIN LOVES PLAYING THE BIG BROTHER. JUSTIN HAS EVEN TWEETED ABOUT HOW MUCH HE ENJOYS SPENDING TIME WITH THEM.

JEREMY JACK BIEBER

Jeremy is Justin's dad and although Jeremy and Pattie split up when Justin was young, they still have a close bond. Jeremy is a self-taught musician and was the one who showed Justin how to play his first chords. He also likes working out in the gym. But these aren't the only father/ son similarities – the two also share a love of tattoos!

BRUCE AND DIANE DALE

Bruce and Diane are Justin's grandparents and Pattie's parents. They are super-close to Justin as they helped raise him when he was young. Bruce and Diane still live in Canada, but Justin always visits when he can!

When Justin turned 18...

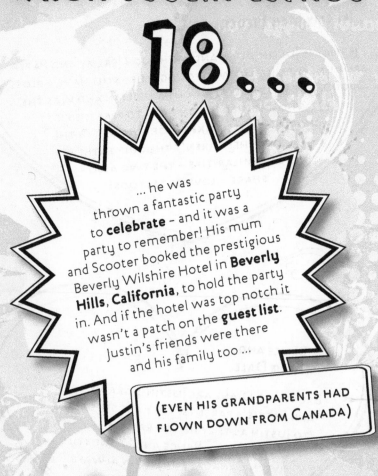

... he was thrown a fantastic party to **celebrate** – and it was a party to remember! His mum and Scooter booked the prestigious Beverly Wilshire Hotel in **Beverly Hills, California**, to hold the party in. And if the hotel was top notch it wasn't a patch on the **guest list**. Justin's friends were there and his family too ...

(EVEN HIS GRANDPARENTS HAD FLOWN DOWN FROM CANADA)

plus there were a load of celebrities.

Which celebrities?

These celebrities!

Miley Cyrus

Jaden and Willow Smith

Mike Tyson – and who knew he was a Belieber???!!!

Taio Cruz

Carly Rae Jepson

Cody Simpson

Ashlee Tisdale

Kim Kardashian

Selena Gomez

When Justin turned 18 he was given the best gift ever from his manager Scooter Braun and his mentor Usher. It was a **super-cool** sports car called a **Fisker Karma**. It's not only fast, but it's good for the planet, too as it's a **hybrid** – which means it uses electric motors as well as a petrol engine to keep the air pollution down.

The car costs about $100,000 (£87,000) so that's one expensive birthday surprise!

And we bet it was impossible to wrap!

JUSTIN HAS A SAYING THAT HE
LIKES TO LIVE HIS LIFE BY.

His motto is:

Never Say Never

Just three little words but ones that open up a
whole world of possibilities. Who would have
thought a kid from Canada could be a huge star
thanks to some home videos? Well if you think
'Never Say Never' then suddenly **ANYTHING**
becomes possible!

Even a super talent like Justin can't run the show on his own. He has a whole team of people to help him conquer the world with his tunes. Here are some of the top people from

Team Bieber:

Vocal Producer:
Kuk Harrell

Manager:
Scott 'Scooter' Braun

Business Manager:
Allison Kaye

Music Director:
Dan Kanter

Stage Manager:
James 'Scrappy' Stacey

Tour Manager:
Kenny Hamilton

Fashion Advice:
Ryan Good

Hair Stylist:
Vanessa Price

Justin also has his good friend Alfredo Flores to rely on, and his mother, Pattie, too.

 # ARE YOU A BIEBER BRAINIAC?

Do you think you know everything about Justin? Then test yourself with our fiendish quiz!

1 WHERE WAS JUSTIN BORN?

LONDON, ENGLAND
LONDON, ONTARIO
LONDON, BURGUNDY
IN THE BACK OF A PICK-UP TRUCK

2 WHAT DID JUSTIN'S DAD DO?

HORSE WHISPERER
LORRY DRIVER
MUSICIAN
ASTRONAUT

3 TRUE OR FALSE?

HIS MIDDLE NAME IS JACK

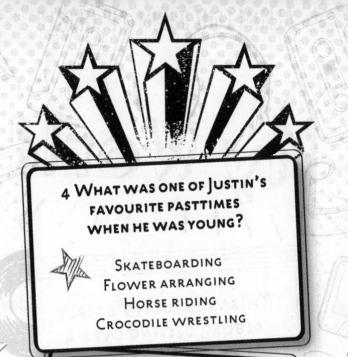

4 WHAT WAS ONE OF JUSTIN'S FAVOURITE PASTTIMES WHEN HE WAS YOUNG?

SKATEBOARDING
FLOWER ARRANGING
HORSE RIDING
CROCODILE WRESTLING

5 WHICH STAR HELPED JUSTIN TO BECOME FAMOUS?

USHER
RIHANNA
KATY PERRY
JAY Z

6 TRUE OR FALSE?

JUSTIN ONCE FOUGHT WITH AN ALSATIAN DOG TO SAVE A BABY!

All answers on pages 90-93

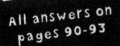

My World

THIS WAS JUSTIN'S FIRST ALBUM, SELLING OVER A MILLION COPIES IN THE UNITED STATES ALONE!

Here's everything you could want to know about it.

RELEASE DATE: 17 NOVEMBER 2009

HIGHEST POSITION IN THE US CHARTS: 5
HIGHEST POSITION IN THE UK CHARTS: 4

TRACK LIST

1. ONE TIME
2. FAVORITE GIRL
3. DOWN TO EARTH
4. BIGGER
5. ONE LESS LONELY GIRL
6. FIRST DANCE
7. LOVE ME
8. COMMON DENOMINATOR
9. ONE LESS LONELY GIRL
   (JB SINGS THIS ONE IN FRENCH–
   FOR THOSE LUCKY CANADIANS)

SINGLES FROM THE ALBUM

1. ONE TIME
2. ONE LESS LONELY GIRL

WE ALL KNOW THAT JUSTIN'S FULL NAME IS JUSTIN DREW BIEBER, BUT THAT'S A BIT OF A MOUTHFUL. SO WHAT DO HIS FRIENDS, FAMILY AND FANS CALL HIM INSTEAD? THESE ARE HIS TOP NICKNAMES.

The Kid

This is what his manager Scooter Braun calls him. Scooter is so close to Justin and his family that Justin thinks of him as being more like an uncle – the sort of uncle that turns you into a global superstar!

JB

Nice and simple this one. Just using the initials makes it quick and snappy. The only downside is that it's not just for Justin, but with anyone with those initials John Brown, Jane Blair...

The Bieb

The one, the only, Justin Bieber; people like the way this nickname sets him apart from everyone else.

Beebs/Biebs

Like calling him The Bieb, but this one sounds a bit more like you know him.

J Beebs/J Biebz

Basically the same nicknames but with different spellings – which style do you prefer?

The Biebernator

Like a cross between Justin and the scary robot from the Terminator films. Of course if Justin was a robot he would be able to keep touring all year round without getting tired!

Do you know any other nicknames?

BIEBER HEROES

JUSTIN HAS INSPIRED MILLIONS OF PEOPLE AROUND THE WORLD, SO IT MIGHT BE SURPRISING THAT SOME PEOPLE INSPIRE HIM. HE HAS HEROES FROM ALL DIFFERENT WALKS OF LIFE AND THESE ARE HIS TOP ONES.

MICHAEL JACKSON

The King of Pop achieved everything Justin would like to. He successfully made the move from child star in the band **The Jackson Five** to being a successful solo artist as an adult. He sold millions of records and his album **Thriller** is still the best-selling album of all time. Michael Jackson was also famous for his dance moves – something Justin is getting a reputation for too!

USHER

The R&B and pop megastar was a hero of Justin's long before he became a friend and mentor. Some of the earliest songs Pattie posted onto **YouTube** were of Justin singing **Usher** songs – maybe it was this that encouraged Usher to sign him. Usher has sold millions of records and won a number of **Grammy awards**. He has also appeared on TV and in movies and does a lot of work for charity.

KOBE BRYANT

Kobe Bryant is one of the most famous and successful basketball players ever. He was the youngest player ever to be named an All Star. He has won five championships with his team the **L.A. Lakers** and has also won two Olympic gold medals. Kobe was also friends with Michael Jackson.

PATTIE MALLET

Justin has bags of respect for his mum (aww!). He knows how hard she had to work when he was young and is thankful that she has given up everything to help him in his career. She was the one who set the example that anything can be achieved with hard work.

Justin and Pattie

When he's not travelling the world on tour Justin likes to take a break with some sports. He loves shooting hoops and running around a basketball court. Justin did athletics at school – which must have got him fit for all those dance moves on stage! He's also tried a bit of boxing!

He was a good **football player** at school and played for the All Star travelling soccer team. But that wasn't the peak of Justin's football career; he actually got the chance to join in a training session with **Barcelona F.C.** - probably the world's best football team - when he was on tour in 2011. Who knows, if the singing hadn't worked out maybe he would have been a **professional** football star!

However, Justin's favourite team in the whole world is an **ice hockey** team. He is a huge Toronto Maple Leafs fan and like lots of Canadians, Justin thinks ice hockey is one of the **best sports ever!**

Being a **perfectionist**, when Justin plays a sport he plays to win – and keeps going until he has. On tour he and his crew played **table tennis** tournaments and Justin wouldn't stop playing until he had beaten everybody. Eventually he did, which is just as well...

In case you're wondering what the young Justin looked like in ice hockey gear!

... Justin admits he's a terrible loser!

My World 2.0

This was Justin's first full-length album and was a follow on to the shorter **My World** album released in 2009. This was where Bieber-mania really took off! The album rocketed to the top of the charts in many countries and sold by the bucketload.

Justin Bieber had arrived - and in style!

RELEASE DATE: 19 MARCH 2010

HIGHEST POSITION IN THE US CHARTS: 1
HIGHEST POSITION IN THE UK CHARTS: 3

TRACK LIST

1 BABY
2 SOMEBODY TO LOVE
3 STUCK IN THE MOMENT
4 U SMILE
5 RUNAWAY LOVE
6 NEVER LET YOU GO
7 OVERBOARD
8 EENIE MEENIE
9 UP
10 THAT SHOULD BE ME

SINGLES FROM THE ALBUM

1 BABY
2 NEVER LET YOU GO
3 EENIE MEENIE
4 SOMEBODY TO LOVE
5 U SMILE

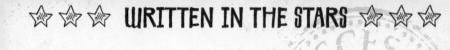
JUSTIN'S DATE OF BIRTH IS THE **1 MARCH 1994** – WHAT DO THE HOROSCOPES MAKE OF THIS IMPORTANT DATE?

According to the signs of the zodiac, Justin is a **Pisces**. Pisces is the sign of the fish and according to astrologers a typical Pisces person is **artistic**, **sensitive** and **thoughtful**. They are also hard working. Anyone who has been lucky enough to see Justin **live on stage** will agree that he knows how to put the effort in.

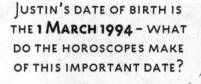

Other famous Pisceans include:

ALBERT EINSTEIN

GEORGE WASHINGTON

CHRIS MARTIN FROM COLDPLAY

RIHANNA

JESSICA BIEL

The Chinese zodiac works on the year of your birth rather than the exact date, and uses 12 different **animals** in order. As Justin was born in 1994 the Chinese zodiac would have him in the **Year of the Dog**. People born in the Year of the Dog are said to be smart, loyal, **courageous** and **lively**.

People born in the year of the dog include:

MICHAEL JACKSON

MADONNA

WINSTON CHURCHILL

ELVIS PRESLEY

PRINCE WILLIAM

THE VIDEO FOR THE SONG **BABY** HAS BEEN VIEWED OVER 800,000,000 (THAT'S EIGHT HUNDRED MILLION) TIMES ON **YOUTUBE**! THAT'S MORE THAN TWICE THE POPULATION OF THE ENTIRE UNITED STATES OF AMERICA, OR MORE THAN 12 TIMES THE POPULATION OF THE UK. IT IS THE SECOND MOST POPULAR VIDEO ON YOUTUBE – LOSING TOP SPOT TO PSY'S **GANGNAM STYLE** IN 2012!

'I totally love Justin - he's just perfect. When he sings I like to think he's talking just to me. I want to marry him!'

Katy, age 12

Disaster!

THE NAMES OF THESE BIEBER SONGS HAVE BECOME ALL MUDDLED UP! CAN YOU WORK OUT WHAT THEY REALLY ARE?

YABB

RENEV YAS VRENE

RYPA

PU

ONRB OT EB
DESYMOBO

LIBEEVE

♫ MOMCNO
TDOEMNIRANO

EDBAORVOR

NOFYIRDBE

MUMDERR YOB

37

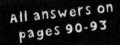
All answers on
pages 90-93

1 Which of Justin's cars is not black?

2 How many cars does Justin own?

3 Which of his cars would Batman like to drive?

4 What is Justin's car colour and finish of choice?

5 Which car does Justin use as a city drive?

6 How did Justin get around before he passed his driving test?!

All answers on pages 90-93

MY WORLDS ACOUSTIC

SAW JUSTIN REMIXING SOME OF THE SONGS FROM HIS FIRST TWO ALBUMS AND PLAYING THEM IN A MUCH MORE LOW-KEY STYLE. THERE WAS ALSO A NEW SONG CALLED **PRAY**. IT WASN'T OFFICIALLY RELEASED EVERYWHERE 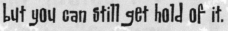 (boo!)

but you can still get hold of it.

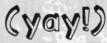 (yay!)

RELEASE DATE: 26 NOVEMBER 2010

HIGHEST POSITION IN THE US CHARTS: 17

TRACK LIST

1	ONE TIME
2	BABY
3	ONE LESS LONELY GIRL
4	DOWN TO EARTH
5	U SMILE
6	STUCK IN THE MOMENT
7	FAVORITE GIRL (LIVE VERSION)
8	THAT SHOULD BE ME
9	NEVER SAY NEVER
10	PRAY

MEET THE BAND

While JB is doing his thing at the front of the stage, his backing band are doing their thing behind him. Justin has played with all sorts of different people and here are some of them:

Dan Kanter
ON GUITAR

Wizard Jones
ON KEYBOARDS

Tomi Martin
ALSO ON GUITAR

Bernard Harvey
ON BASS GUITAR

Melvin Baldwin
ON DRUMS

DJ Tay James
ON THE DECKS

Justin's backing singers are called...

Legaci

Tattoos aren't everyone's cup of tea but at the time of publication Justin has 11 of them on various bits of his body.

1 BIRD
Apparently this is meant to be a flying seagull from the book, **Jonathan Livingston Seagull**. This was Justin's first tattoo. It's on his hip.

2 THE WORD 'YESHUA'
This is the Hebrew word for **Jesus**. JB is a Christian and got this tattoo when he was in Israel. His dad got the same one at the same time, too.

3 PICTURE OF JESUS
This one is on his left leg.

4 PRAYING HANDS WITH ROSES
This one is also on his left leg. If he's been praying for success it certainly worked.

5 THE WORD 'BELIEVE'
This one's on his left arm and is handy if he ever forgets the name of one of his albums.

6 JAPANESE SYMBOL
On his right arm this time and the symbol means 'music'.

7 CROWN
The crown is on Justin's chest. Could he be the next King of Pop?

8 OWL
There's a big owl on his left arm. **What a hoot!**

9 NATIVE AMERICAN
There's the head of a Native American on Justin's left shoulder.

10 ROMAN NUMBERS
Justin has the Roman numerals for his Mum's birthdate on his chest, too. Or maybe it's his pin number?!

11 CROSS
There's cross on his left arm which is actually the Greek letter for 'Christ'.

TATTOOS ARE PERMANENT AND WON'T JUST FADE AWAY. YOU CANNOT GET A TATTOO UNTIL YOU ARE 18 YEARS OLD - SO IT'S BEST TO STICK TO THE TEMPORARY ONES!

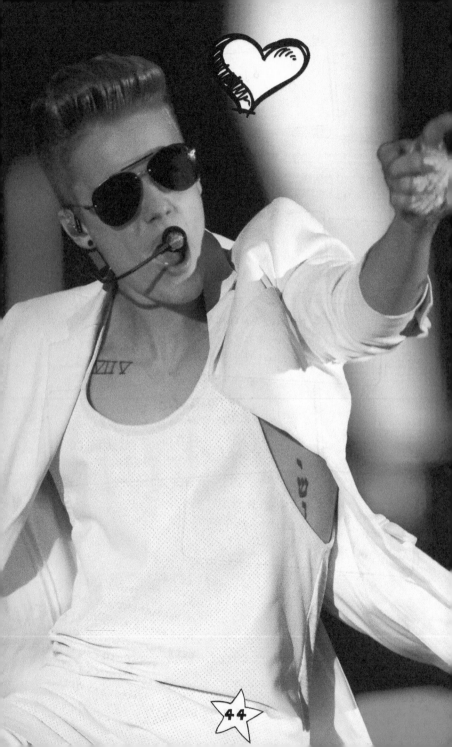

'A beautiful smile, beautiful eyes and a good sense of humour. She should be honest, loving and trustworthy.'

JUSTIN TALKS ABOUT WHAT HE LIKES IN A GIRLFRIEND.

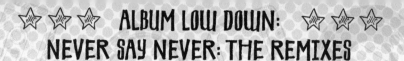

FOLLOWING THE SUCCESS OF **MY WORLD: ACOUSTIC** JUSTIN RELEASED ANOTHER REMIX ALBUM CALLED **NEVER SAY NEVER: THE REMIXES**. THIS TIME THE ALBUM WASN'T ACOUSTIC VERSIONS OF THE SONGS THOUGH AND WAS RELEASED TO TIE IN WITH JUSTIN'S FIRST FILM – ALSO CALLED **NEVER SAY NEVER**. THERE WAS A BRAND NEW SONG ON THE ALBUM, TOO, AND ALSO LOADS OF FAMOUS SINGERS JOINED JUSTIN TO GIVE HIS SONGS A NEW FLAVOUR!

RELEASE DATE: 14 FEBRUARY 2011

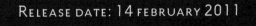

HIGHEST POSITION IN THE US CHARTS: 1
HIGHEST POSITION IN THE UK CHARTS: 17

TRACK LIST

1   NEVER SAY NEVER
    (WITH JADEN SMITH)

2   THAT SHOULD BE ME
    (WITH RASCAL FLATTS)

3   SOMEBODY TO LOVE
    (WITH USHER)

4   UP
    (WITH CHRIS BROWN)

5   OVERBOARD
    (WITH MILEY CYRUS)

6   RUNAWAY LOVE
    (WITH KANYE WEST AND RAEKWON)

7   BORN TO BE SOMEBODY

SINGLES FROM THE ALBUM

1   NEVER SAY NEVER

✦ ✦ ✦ MUSIC MAN QUIZ ✦ ✦ ✦

JB TAUGHT HIMSELF
TO PLAY SOME MUSICAL
INSTRUMENTS, BUT DO YOU KNOW
WHICH ONES? CHECK OUT THE
LIST BELOW AND TEST YOUR
KNOWLEDGE!

drums

banjo

harmonica

tuba

violin

guitar

piano

trumpet

vibraphone

48

All answers on pages 90-93

TICKET

JUSTIN'S DOCUMENTARY-STYLE FILM **NEVER SAY NEVER** SHOWED THE BUILD-UP TO JUSTIN'S SOLD OUT CONCERT AT **MADISON SQUARE GARDEN** IN 2010 THE CONCERT WAS A SUPER HIT. BUT HOW MUCH OF A HIT WAS THE FILM?

WELL, IT TOOK MORE MONEY IN CINEMAS IN THE USA THAN ANY OTHER CONCERT FILM, EVER! IT TOOK OVER $25.5 MILLION (£16.5 MILLION) ON ITS OPENING WEEKEND AND OVER $73 MILLION (£43 MILLION) IN THE USA ALONE. ADD IN THE $25 MILLION (£16 MILLION) FROM THE TAKINGS FROM THE REST OF THE WORLD THAT GIVES A GRAND TOTAL OF VERY NEARLY...

$99 million

(that's £64 million)!

JUSTIN HAS BEEN LUCKY ENOUGH TO SING WITH BIG STARS BOTH ON STAGE AND IN THE RECORDING STUDIO. SOME OF THEM ARE FRIENDS, OR PEOPLE THAT HAVE HELPED JB'S CAREER; OTHERS SIMPLY KNOW THAT JUSTIN IS A GREAT ARTIST TO WORK WITH!

But who was cool enough to collaborate with Justin?

Have a look for yourself:

USHER	LUDACRIS

MARIAH CAREY	SEAN KINGSTON	BOYZ II MEN
NICKI MINAJ	BUSTA RHYMES	JADEN SMITH
CARLY RAE JEPSEN	KANYE WEST	TAYLOR SWIFT
CARLOS SANTANA	WILL.I.AM	LIL TWIST
CHRIS BROWN	RASCAL FLATTS	RAEKWON

There have also been rumours of collaborations with all sorts of different artists including **Maroon 5**, **Cody Simpson** and **One Direction**. There's even been talk of a partnership with **Slipknot's Corey Taylor**! We can't wait to hear that.

Justin and
Sean Kingston
do their thing.

Who would you like to see Justin collaborating with?

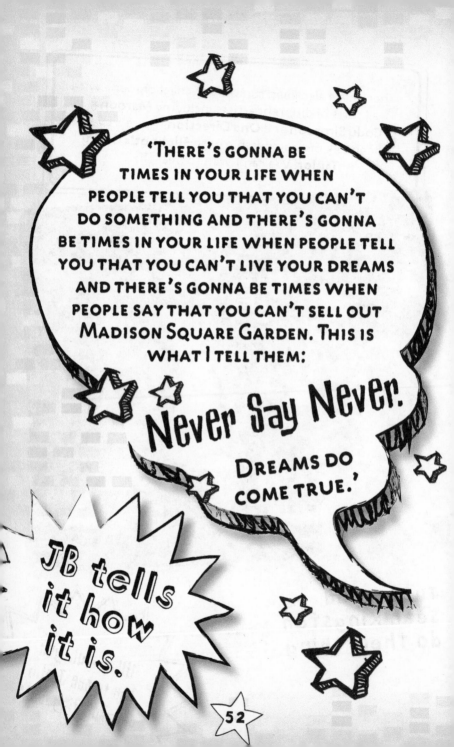

'THERE'S GONNA BE TIMES IN YOUR LIFE WHEN PEOPLE TELL YOU THAT YOU CAN'T DO SOMETHING AND THERE'S GONNA BE TIMES IN YOUR LIFE WHEN PEOPLE TELL YOU THAT YOU CAN'T LIVE YOUR DREAMS AND THERE'S GONNA BE TIMES WHEN PEOPLE SAY THAT YOU CAN'T SELL OUT MADISON SQUARE GARDEN. THIS IS WHAT I TELL THEM:

Never Say Never.

DREAMS DO COME TRUE.'

JB tells it how it is.

WANT TO KNOW WHAT JUSTIN LIKES?

Here are a few of his favourite things:

Favourite food:
spaghetti Bolognese

Favourite ice cream:
dulce con leche con brownie (toffee ice cream with brownie chunks)

Favourite sweets:
sour patch kids, sour skittles, watermelon sour patch (sounds like JB's sweet tooth isn't that sweet)

Favourite film:
Rocky IV

Favourite school subject:
English Literature

Favourite sports team:
Toronto Maple Leafs

Favourite TV show:
Smallville

Favourite video game:
Mortal Combat

Favourite songs:
Man in the Mirror by Michael Jackson,
On Bended Knee by Boyz II Men

☆☆☆ ALBUM LOW DOWN: ☆☆☆
MY WORLDS: THE COLLECTIONS

THIS WAS A DOUBLE ALBUM THAT COMBINED THE TRACKS FROM THE FIRST THREE **MY WORLD** ALBUMS PLUS THE EXTRA TRACKS **PRAY, NEVER SAY NEVER,** AND **SOMEBODY TO LOVE**. SOME OF THE TRACKS WERE ACOUSTIC, OR LIVE, OR EVEN REMIXED VERSIONS OF THE SONGS WE ALL KNOW.

RELEASE DATE: 19 NOVEMBER 2010

TRACK LIST

DISC ONE

1   ONE TIME
2   BABY
3   ONE LESS LONELY GIRL
4   DOWN TO EARTH
5   U SMILE
6   STUCK IN THE MOMENT
7   FAVORITE GIRL
8   THAT SHOULD BE ME
9   NEVER SAY NEVER
10 PRAY
11 SOMEBODY TO LOVE
12 NEVER SAY NEVER
13 SOMEBODY TO LOVE

SOMETIMES THERE WERE EVEN DIFFERENT VERSIONS
OF THE SAME SONG ON THE ALBUM. IT HAD A
LIMITED RELEASE IN A FEW EUROPEAN COUNTRIES.

DISC TWO

1 ONE TIME
2 FAVORITE GIRL
3 DOWN TO EARTH
4 BIGGER
5 ONE LESS LONELY GIRL
6 FIRST DANCE
7 LOVE ME
8 COMMON DENOMINATOR
9 BABY
10 SOMEBODY TO LOVE
11 STUCK IN THE MOMENT
12 U SMILE
13 RUNAWAY LOVE
14 NEVER LET YOU GO
15 OVERBOARD
16 EENIE MEENIE
17 UP
18 THAT SHOULD BE ME

SINGLES FROM THE ALBUM

1 PRAY

Can you guess who is being described here?

The clue is that they're all important people in Justin's life — but can you work out who they are?

1 Justin describes him as being like an uncle. He's a tough negotiator and has steered Justin from little-known Canadian teenager to **global superstar**. His name might sound like some kind of toy, but he makes sure that Justin's working hard.

2 He's been overseeing Justin's career from the start offering advice and **collaborating** with him in the studio and on stage. He's one of Justin's close friends and advisors – and a huge star in his own right.

3 This talented lady first game to the public's attention as an actress in **Wizards of Waverly Place**. She's also a singer and a designer and was one of Justin's most high profile girlfriends.

4 Described by many as the 'King of Pop' this **megastar** was perhaps the biggest recording artist in history. Like Justin, this **mystery person** started out as a child star and went on to conquer the world. He's one of Justin's all-time idols.

5 She's the most special lady in Justin's life and often accompanies him to **award ceremonies** and **parties**. She knows JB better than anyone else in the entire world.

6 This group of people are really important to Justin and in many ways his success is down to them – without them JB would still be a teenager singing songs on **YouTube**.

57

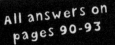All answers on pages 90-93

JB'S HAIRSTYLES ARE SO FAMOUS THEY COULD ALMOST HAVE CAREERS OF THEIR OWN. ALTHOUGH HE'S CHANGED HIS LOOK A FEW TIMES THEY ARE BASICALLY RE-INVENTIONS OF JUST TWO BASIC STYLES:

1. The side-sweep

Justin's original do, his brushed-down barnet was the cut that the world was introduced to at the very start of his career. The flat, side-swept style looked cute on the younger Justin!

2. The spiked-up

Justin's current style, it's cropped closer to the side and the back and spiked up at the front and top. It's a much-copied style and is a flattering look. More to the point it helps mark the difference between the younger and older Justin.

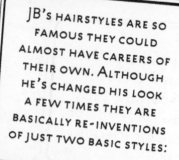

Which one do you prefer?

Justin spends lots of time on the road touring and playing gigs. This can be exhausting at the best of times!

But especially as Justin gives everything to his dance routines. No one figured out quite how dangerous it could be.

In 2009 Justin was singing at Wembley Arena, London and managed to break his foot! He kept singing though - the show must go on. He didn't cancel his tour or anything and performed the next 14 gigs wearing a plaster cast!

What a superstar!

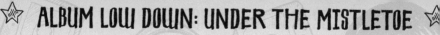

Feeling festive?

IF YOU ARE, THEN THIS CHRISTMAS ALBUM IS JUST WHAT YOU NEED! SOME OF HIS CELEBRITY FRIENDS SANG WITH HIM, INCLUDING **USHER** AND **BUSTA RHYMES** AND **MARIAH CAREY**. MANY ARTISTS ARE WORRIED ABOUT RELEASING A CHRISTMAS ALBUM AS THEY TEND NOT TO SELL VERY WELL. THAT WASN'T THE CASE WITH JUSTIN'S FESTIVE RELEASE THOUGH – IT WAS A GLOBAL HIT AND CHARTED AT NUMBER 1 IN A NUMBER OF COUNTRIES.

Merry Christmas Justin!

RELEASE DATE: 1 NOVEMBER 2011

HIGHEST POSITION IN THE US CHARTS: 1
HIGHEST POSITION IN THE UK CHARTS: 14

TRACK LIST

1   THE ONLY THING I EVER GET
    FOR CHRISTMAS
2   MISTLETOE
3   THE CHRISTMAS SONG
    (CHESTNUTS ROASTING ON AN OPEN FIRE)
4   SANTA CLAUS IS COMING TO TOWN
5   FA LA LA
6   ALL I WANT FOR CHRISTMAS IS YOU
    (SUPER FESTIVE!)
7   DRUMMER BOY
8   CHRISTMAS EVE
9   ALL I WANT IS YOU
10 HOME THIS CHRISTMAS
11 SILENT NIGHT

BONUS TRACKS ON THE DELUXE EDITION

12 CHRISTMAS LOVE
13 LA LA (CAPELLA VERSION)
14 PRAY
15 SOMEDAY AT CHRISTMAS

SINGLES FROM THE ALBUM

1   MISTLETOE

Being a global superstar has some downsides and these can be difficult to deal with ...

Justin has been a **celebrity** since he was a teenager and he has done his **growing up** in the public eye. Every time something goes wrong the **newspapers** and Internet are onto the story. Sometimes stories are exaggerated or even made up about him!

Worse still is the lack of **privacy**. Justin is never alone. He can't go to the shops or hang with his friends without it being a big event! You can't really blame Justin's fans though – they just want to catch a glimpse of their **fave pop star**. Justin realizes this, too and knowing they are there for him makes him feel good. To give Justin a bit of space they give him privacy and let him get on with things...

...and he really appreciates it!

Worst of all are the **paparazzi** – professional photographers who sell their images to the newspapers. They don't really care about Justin, they just want a **good picture** and will go to any lengths to get one!

Whenever he goes out they follow him – even **chasing him** in cars! One time JB fancied an ice cream and the only way he could eat it without being photographed...

...was to hide in the boot of his car!

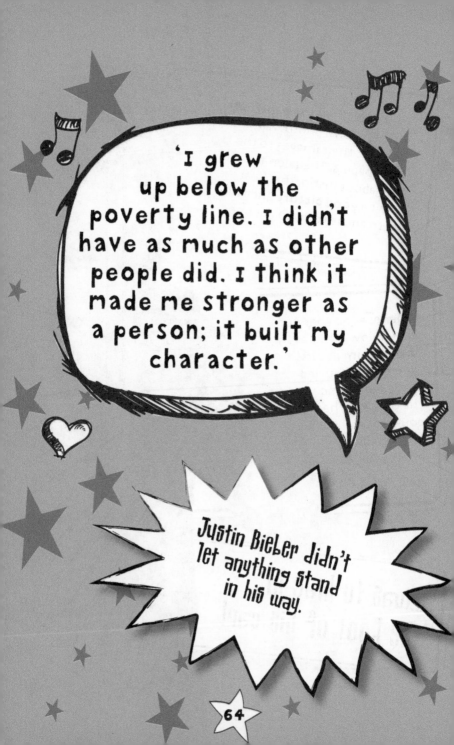

'I grew up below the poverty line. I didn't have as much as other people did. I think it made me stronger as a person; it built my character.'

Justin Bieber didn't let anything stand in his way.

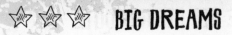
Even Justin Bieber has big dreams and things he has yet to achieve!

But what are they?

There's one thing Justin would like above all others and that's a **Grammy award**. The Grammys are awarded by The National Academy of Recording Arts and Sciences and are the biggest **music awards** on the planet. Unbelievably JB has never won one!

Another of Justin's dreams is to sing at **the Superbowl**, American football's big finale, during the half-time show. **Millions** of people across the world watch this and some of the biggest names in the music business have sung there, including **Madonna** and **Beyoncé**.

Justin also fancies singing at zero gravity! So much so that he's signed up to take a trip on the Virgin Galactic commercial Space flight. Other celebrities that may be his fellow passengers include **Tom Hanks**, **Leonardo DiCaprio** and **Brad Pitt**!

You've read most of the book, now do you have the knowledge to answer these brain-teasers?

Easy-Peasy...

1. What is Justin's middle name?

2. Where was he born?

3. What was his first single called?

4. What was the name of Justin's film?

Getting Tricky...

5. What tattoo did the Bieb get first?

6. How long did it take to sell out Madison Square Garden in 2010?

7. Which two music megastars tried to get Justin to join their record label?

8. Name three singers Justin covered in his early YouTube videos?

The Tough Ones

9. WHO IS RUMOURED TO BE COLLABORATING WITH JUSTIN IN THE FUTURE?

10. WHAT ARE THE TATTOOS THAT JUSTIN HAS ON HIS LEFT LEG?

11. WHICH VIDEO HAS TAKEN OVER THE TOP SPOT ON YOUTUBE FROM JUSTIN?

12. WHAT AWARD DOES JUSTIN REALLY WANT TO WIN?

All answers on pages 90-93

True or False?

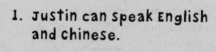

1. Justin can speak English and Chinese.

2. Justin is a Pisces.

3. He was born in the Year of the Goat.

4. Justin is an Internet sensation.

5. His favourite recording artist of all time is Madonna.

6. Justin's mentor is Louis Walsh.

7. Justin has a tattoo of a bird.

8. The star's first film was Never Say Always.

9. His favourite film is Rocky IV.

10. Justin has won three Grammys.

Random

1. What are the names of Justin's half-brother and sister?

2. What type of car did Usher and Scooter buy him?

3. How old was Justin when he was given a car as a birthday present?

4. How many copies did Justin's first album sell?

5. How many times has Baby been viewed on YouTube?

6. What is Justin's motto?

All answers on pages 90-93

That Justin is claustrophobic? – he doesn't like being in closed spaces as it makes him uncomfortable.

When Justin was playing a gig in Hong Kong, the famous Chinese actor and martial arts legend Jackie Chan sent him flowers.

Justin can speak French as well as English. Much of Canada is French-speaking so speaking both languages makes sense when he goes back home.

A school tutor used to tour with Justin – even global megastars need to learn algebra!

Justin's first trip outside of Canada was to meet up with Scooter Braun in Atlanta.

Justin has recorded two songs for his mum. The first was **Mama** by Boyz II Men and the second was **Turn to You** which he wrote.

Justin Timberlake tried to sign Justin to his record label, but he chose Scooter and Usher's label instead.

JUSTIN ISN'T JUST A SUCCESS STORY IN THE MUSIC WORLD – HE'S GOT OTHER STRINGS TO HIS BOW, TOO.

Justin released two perfumes called **Someday** in 2011 and **Girlfriend** in 2012. Someday was the bestselling perfume in the world when it was released in 2011.

Looks like there are a lot of people out there that want a little dab of Bieber on them. **Someday** even won a prize – called a **FiFi Award** – which is big news in the fragrance industry.

If the music ever loses its appeal there's a whole new industry just waiting for him.

Did you know Justin got married?

Take it easy, don't panic!

We don't mean properly married, but he played at being married with a six year old who was ill with a rare cancer. When JB heard of Avalanna Routh's cancer he flew the young fan to New York on Valentine's Day and spent an afternoon playing games and eating cupcakes. They even 'got pretend married'. She loved the day and JB found it pretty emotional. He later tweeted:

'#MrsBieber really inspired me'.

ONE OF JUSTIN'S **COOLEST** DAYS OUT WAS WHEN HE WAS INVITED TO THE WHITE HOUSE IN WASHINGTON TO MEET THE **PRESIDENT OF THE USA,** BARACK OBAMA AND HIS FAMILY!

JUSTIN TOOK PART IN A CHRISTMAS CONCERT AT **THE WHITE HOUSE** IN 2009 AND IT WAS ONE OF THE FEW TIMES HE'S FELT REALLY NERVOUS BEFORE A GIG. HE SANG THE STEVIE WONDER SONG **SOMEDAY AT CHRISTMAS** AND IT WENT DOWN A STORM.

THE NEXT YEAR HE WAS INVITED BACK TO THE WHITE HOUSE, THIS TIME AT EASTER. HE TOOK PART IN THE ANNUAL **EASTER EGG HUNT** AND THEN GOT TO MEET THE PRESIDENT AND HIS FAMILY AND CHAT FOR A WHILE!

'I've spent hours studying Michael Jackson's moves. If I can be even half the performer he was, I'll be happy.'

JUSTIN BIEBER TALKING ABOUT HIS HERO IN HIS BOOK JUST GETTING STARTED (2012)

We think he's there already!

Anyone who's seen Justin move on stage knows he's a great dancer, but if he thinks he can get even better then...

...we're all in for a treat!

THIS AMAZING ALBUM FROM 2012 WAS JAM-PACKED WITH BRAND NEW MATERIAL. HIS MOST GROWN-UP ALBUM TO DATE, JUSTIN EXPERIMENTS WITH DIFFERENT SORTS OF MUSIC – AND NAILS IT! IF JUSTIN HAD WONDERED HOW PEOPLE WOULD REACT TO HIS FRESH NEW SOUND HE NEEDN'T HAVE WORRIED – THE ALBUM WAS A WORLD-WIDE SMASH HIT, TOPPING THE CHARTS IN MORE COUNTRIES THAN EVER BEFORE!

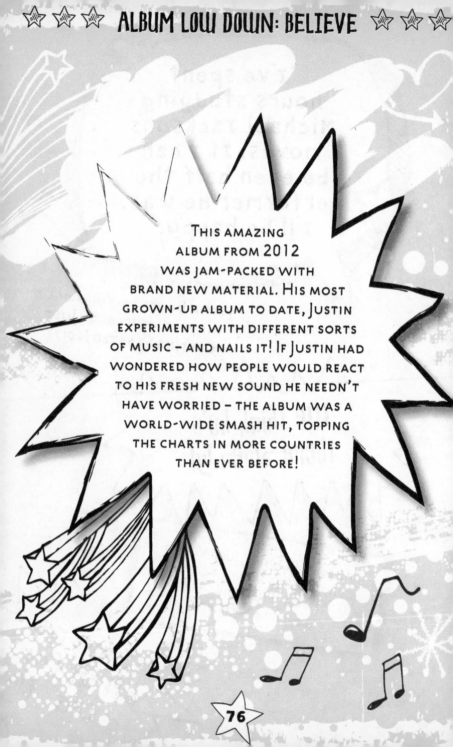

Release date: 15 June 2012
Highest position in the US charts: 1
Highest position in the UK charts: 1

Track List:

1 All Around the World
2 Boyfriend
3 As Long as You Love Me
4 Take You
5 Right Here
6 Catching Feelings
7 Fall
8 Die in Your Arms
9 Thought of You
10 Beauty and a Beat
11 One Love
12 Be Alright
13 Believe

Bonus Tracks
14 Out of Town Girl
15 She Don't Like the Lights
16 Maria

Singles from the album:
1 Boyfriend
2 As Long as You Love Me
3 Beauty and a Beat
4 Right Here

POSSIBLY THE BEST THING ABOUT JUSTIN (OTHER THAN HIS SINGING/DANCING/STYLE) IS THAT HE KNOWS SOME PEOPLE ARE LESS FORTUNATE THAN HE IS – AND HE TRIES TO DO SOMETHING ABOUT IT.

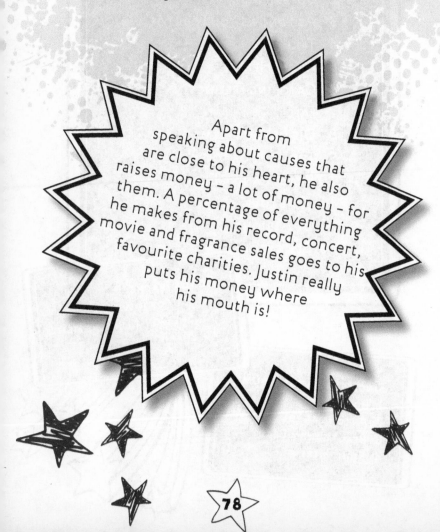

Apart from speaking about causes that are close to his heart, he also raises money – a lot of money – for them. A percentage of everything he makes from his record, concert, movie and fragrance sales goes to his favourite charities. Justin really puts his money where his mouth is!

Justin has raised money for loads of good causes including:

Pencils of Promise that helps build new schools.

Make a Wish Foundation that helps children with life-threatening illnesses.

Project Mediashare for Haiti that sends aid to Haiti.

Children's Miracle Network that helps ill children and children's hospitals.

ON HIS 17TH AND 18TH BIRTHDAYS JB ASKED FANS NOT TO SEND HIM GIFTS, BUT TO DONATE TO A WATER CHARITY INSTEAD.

Justin's own **Believe** charity drive – where he gave proceeds from the song **Mistletoe** and encouraged fans to donate – raised over $1 million (£644,000).

When he's on tour Justin visits his fans in hospitals to brighten their day. Time is tight when on tour, but Justin always makes the effort to give back!

79

✰ ✰ ✰ WHERE IN THE WORLD? ✰ ✰ ✰

Justin is always on tour and not just in the states but all around the world

– THAT'S THE THING ABOUT BEING A **GLOBAL MEGASTAR**. HE PROBABLY SPENDS MORE TIME IN THE AIR THAN HE DOES ON THE GROUND. CHECK OUT THE COUNTRIES HE'S VISITED:

Argentina

Australia

Belgium

Canada

Brazil

Chile

Denmark

Germany

France

Hong Kong

Indonesia

Ireland

Israel

Italy

Japan

Malaysia

Mexico

Netherlands

Philippines

Peru

Spain

Singapore

Switzerland

Taiwan

United Kingdom

Venezuela

It's mega-important that Justin doesn't forget his passport!

AT THE START OF JUSTIN'S CAREER HE GOT A MASSIVE BOOST FROM THE SUPPORT, ADVICE AND TIME THAT USHER GAVE HIM. USHER BECAME HIS MENTOR AND FRIEND; AND WROTE AND RECORDED SONGS WITH HIM.

Justin may well have become super-famous without Usher's input (and no one works harder than JB to make his career a success!), but Usher certainly helped him to succeed quickly.

Justin has always been grateful for the role Usher has played – so much so he's doing it now himself. He is acting as adviser and mentor to fellow Canadian, **Carly Rae Jepsen**. JB first heard Carly on the radio and tweeted about her, later she flew to Los Angeles to meet him and Scooter, and joined their record label.

If the success of CALL ME BABY is anything to go by, then hopefully carly can be the next big thing from canada.

IF THERE'S ONE THING JUSTIN HAS SEEN A LOT OF IT'S HOTEL ROOMS. BUT ONE HOTEL PULLED OUT ALL THE STOPS AND TURNED JUSTIN'S THREE-NIGHT STAY INTO AN ADVENTURE!

The first night Justin arrived at the W Hotel in Mexico City they had set up a basketball court in his room –

that's one BIG room!

The next night when he returned the hoop had gone and there was a boxing ring in there instead!

On the final night the ring had gone and a beach was in its place – with sand and palm trees and Hawaiian music!

THE HOTEL HAD GONE TO THE TROUBLE TO FIND OUT ALL OF JB'S FAVOURITE THINGS JUST TO MAKE HIS STAY MORE FUN –

We bet he looks in there again!

1. JUSTIN HAS A PET DONKEY CALLED USHER.

2. JUSTIN IS A BIG BASKETBALL FAN.

3. THERE'S A STREET IN STRATFORD, ONTARIO CALLED BIEBER DRIVE NAMED AFTER JUSTIN.

4. JUSTIN BEGAN PLAYING INSTRUMENTS AT THREE YEARS OLD.

5. THE WAX USED TO MAKE HIS DUMMY AT MADAME TUSSAUDS WAS ORIGINALLY FROM THE MELTED DOWN DUMMY OF ABRAHAM LINCOLN.

6. LADY GAGA HAS MORE TWITTER FOLLOWERS THAN JUSTIN.

7. JUSTIN BIEBER HAS TWO LEFT FEET!

8. JUSTIN SOLD OUT MADISON SQUARE GARDEN IN 22 MINUTES IN 2010.

9. JUSTIN PLANS TO BE THE FIRST POP STAR TO PLAY A CONCERT ON THE MOON.

10. JUSTIN ONCE BEAT MIKE TYSON IN A BOXING MATCH!

All answers on pages 90-93

AND THE WINNER IS ... JUSTIN BIEBER!

THE MILLIONS OF BELIEBERS OUT
THERE THINK JUSTIN IS JUST
BRILLIANT, BUT DO OTHER PEOPLE
THINK SO TOO? JUDGING BY HIS
AWARDS IT WOULD SEEM SO.

By early 2013 he had won:

2
MTV Video Awards

8
Billboard Music Awards

7
American Music Awards

3
Juno Awards

11
Teen choice Awards

7
MTV Europe Awards

4
Teen Icon Awards

5
Much Music Video Awards

1
VH1 Do Something Award

1
Brit Award

3
Nickleodeon Kids' choice Awards

2
NRJ Music Awards

OF COURSE THE BIG MISS IS A GRAMMY AWARD. WHEN JUSTIN DIDN'T GET ANY NOMINATIONS (WHAT?!) FOR THE 2013 AWARDS

Scooter angrily tweeted:

'I JUST PLAIN DISAGREE. THE KID DESERVED IT. THE KID DELIVERED. HUGE SUCCESSFUL ALBUM, SOLD OUT TOUR, AND WON PEOPLE OVER.'

Did you know you can see Justin in **London** any time you like. You can see him in **New York** at the same time, too. But how is this possible – has Justin mastered the art of time travel as well as making a best-selling track? Well no, he's not that good – what you're seeing is a **waxwork**.

The models are at the Madame Tussauds attractions in both cities. The models look pretty good as Madame Tussauds goes to great lengths to make the models look as realistic as possible. The people making the dummy even asked Justin's hair stylist for tips on how to get the hair looking just right.

If you can't meet Justin in real life this might be the next best thing!

Albums

My World
My World 2.0
My World Acoustic
My World Collection
Never Say Never
Under the Mistletoe
Believe

Film

Never Say Never

Books

First Step 2 Forever: My Story
The Official Justin Bieber Poster Book
The Official Justin Bieber Scrap Book
Just Getting Started

Websites and Fan Clubs

HTTP://BIEBERFEVER.COM/
HTTP://WWW.JUSTINBIEBERMUSIC.COM/

Social Media

Twitter: @JUSTINBIEBER

ANSWERS TO THE QUIZ QUESTIONS

So how did you get on with the quizzes? Are you a true Belieber or more of a casual fan? It's the moment of truth, so check the answers and find out!

Pages 20-21
Are you a Bieber Brainiac?
1. London, Ontario
2. Musician
3. False
4. Skateboarding
5. Usher
6. False – but we're sure he would!

Pages 36-37
Song Shuffle Shake Up
Baby
Never Say Never
Pray
Up
Born to be Somebody
Believe
Common Denominator
Overboard
Boyfriend
Drummer Boy

ANSWERS TO THE QUIZ QUESTIONS

PAGES 38-39
CAR QUIZ
1. HIS FISKER KARMA. IT IS CHROME
2. HE HAS 8 CARS
3. BATMAN WOULD BE AT HOME IN THE CADILLAC CTS-V!
4. JUSTIN LOVES MATT BLACK CARS
5. THE SMART CAR IS PERFECT FOR NIPPING AROUND THE CITY
6. HE RODE HIS SKATEBOARD!

PAGE 48
MUSIC MAN QUIZ
JUSTIN CAN PLAY:
DRUMS
TRUMPET
PIANO
GUITAR

PAGE 56-57
GUESS WHO?
1. SCOOTER BRAUN
2. USHER
3. SELENA GOMEZ
4. MICHAEL JACKSON
5. PATTIE MALLETTE
6. YOU, THE FANS

ANSWERS TO THE QUIZ QUESTIONS

Pages 66-67
The Big Bieber Quiz

Easy Peasy
1. Drew
2. London, Ontario
3. One Time
4. Never Say Never

Getting tricky
5. A seagull
6. 22 minutes
7. Usher and Justin Timberlake
8. Usher, Stevie Wonder and Ne-Yo

The tough ones
9. Maroon 5, Cody Simpson, One Direction and Corey Taylor
10. Jesus and praying hands with roses
11. PSY's Gangnam Style
12. A Grammy award

Page 68
TRUE OR FALSE

1. False
2. True
3. False
4. True
5. False!
6. False
7. True

8. FALSE
9. TRUE
10. FALSE

PAGE 69
RANDOM

1. JUSTIN'S HALF-BROTHER AND HALF-SISTER ARE CALLED JAXON AND JAZMYN.
2. THEY BOUGHT HIM A FISKER KARMA.
3. HE WAS 18 WHEN HE GOT THE CAR.
4. JUSTIN'S FIRST ALBUM SOLD OVER ONE MILLION COPIES WORLDWIDE.
5. BABY HAS BEEN VIEWED 800 MILLION TIMES ON YOUTUBE!
6. HIS FAVOURITE SAYING IS NEVER SAY NEVER

PAGE 84-85
TRUE OR FALSE

1. FALSE
2. TRUE
3. FALSE
4. TRUE
5. FALSE
6. TRUE
7. FALSE
8. TRUE
9. FALSE
10. FALSE

⭐ ⭐ INDEX ⭐ ⭐

Congratulations!

Now you really, truly **KNOW** your idol
(probably better than his own mum).
But what about your **OTHER** idols, like
One Direction, **Olly Murs**, **Katy Perry**,
Robert Pattinson and **James Arthur**?

WHAT ABOUT THEM...?

DON'T
PANIC.

Simply check out the other titles
in the series and become an

EVEN
BIGGER
FAN.

Want to Know Your Idol?

TOTALLY AWESOME TITLES IN THE SERIES:

9780750279321

9780750279338

9780750279307

9780750279314

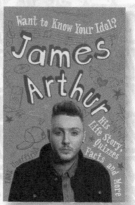

9780750278386

9780750278362

WHY NOT COLLECT THEM ALL?